• MEET •
OHARA KOSON

Read With You Center for
Excellence in STEAM Education

Read With You

Lapwing and Reed, undated

Frog and Tadpoles, undated

Two Cockatoos and Plum Blossom, 1925-1936

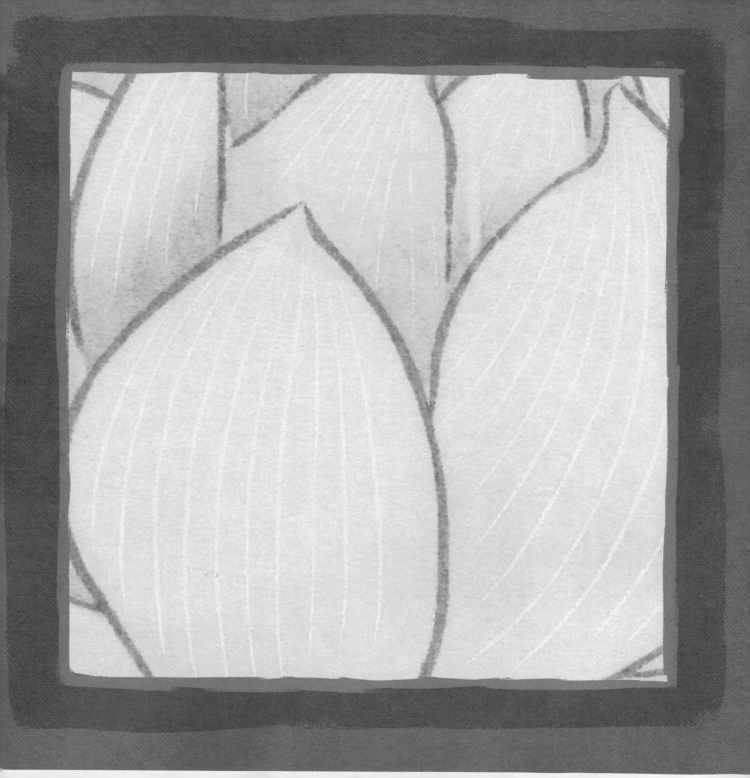

Kingfisher with Lotus Flower, undated

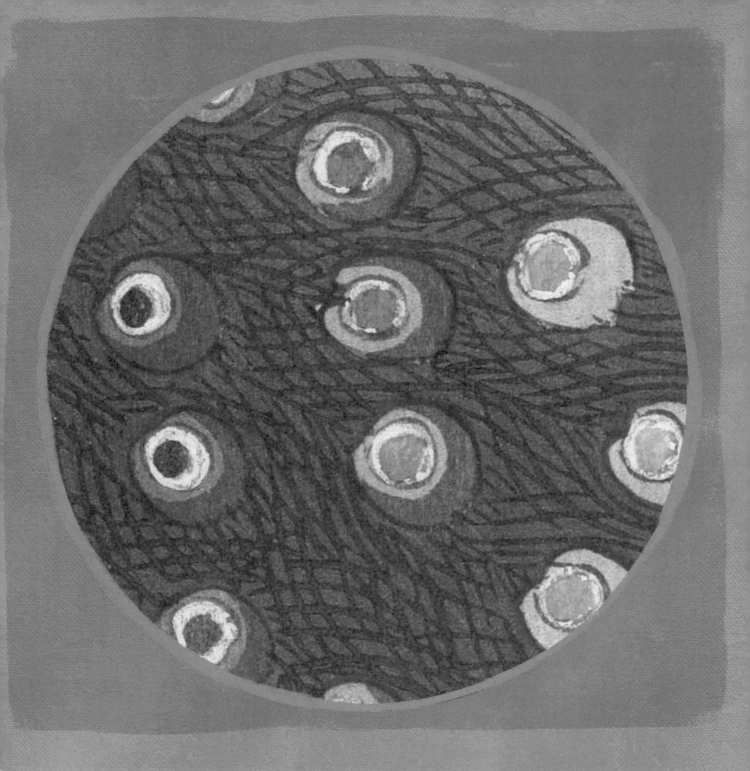

Peacock on a Cherry Blossom Tree, undated

Grass and Flowers at Full Moon, undated

Siberian Blue Nightingale with a Peony under a Snowy Sheaf, 1931-1936

Monkey Hanging on Bamboo Branch, undated

Find Examples

This print is *Peacock* (1925–1936). *Kachō-e* prints like these are made by carving different layers onto wooden blocks and stamping one color at a time onto paper.

Count the colors in this picture. How many wooden blocks did Ohara Koson need for this print?

Which other part of the peacock uses the same color as its beak?

Which color was used the most? Which color was used the least?

Connect

This painting is titled *Great Spotted Woodpecker in Tree with Red Ivy* (1925-1936).

Why is the ivy red?

What kind of feathers can you see clearly on the woodpecker? Which are hidden?

What might Ohara have painted on the tree if it was a different season?

If you were making a *kachō-e* print, what bird or flower would you use?

Craft

Option 1

1. Ask an adult for a foam cube and a chopstick. Use the chopstick to carve a small picture into the cube.

2. Use a foam brush to cover the foam cube with a thin layer of paint, then press the cube against a paper.

3. Keep using this stamp to make a design or create new stamps to try!

Option 2

1. Choose one flower from this book. Draw it by drawing the petals in front first and slowly moving backward toward the most hidden petals.

2. Then, choose one bird from this book. Draw it next to your flower, creating the outline first and filling it in with feathers from the top of the bird's head down to the tops of its legs.

3. Color in your picture with only two or three colors.